PROHIBITING *TAKFIR*
Fatwas of Shi'i Scholars

A TRANSLATION OF
*Hormat Ahanat va Takfir-e
Mosalmanan az Didgah-e 'Olama-ye Shi'eh*

COMPILED BY
Secretariat of the Congress on the Danger of Extremist and Takfirist Currents

TRANSLATED BY
Ahmed Haneef

British Library Cataloguing-in-Publication Data
A catalogue record for this book is available from the British Library.

ISBN: 978-1-904934-30-1 (pbk)

© ISLAMIC CENTRE OF ENGLAND, 2018
This edition first published in 2018.

All rights reserved.

The Islamic Centre of England
140 Maida Vale, London W9 1QB
www.ic-el.com

Contents

Preface 5
Introduction 6
Imam Khomeini 8
Grand Ayatollah Sayyid 'Ali Khamene'i 10
Grand Ayatollah Nasir Makarim Shirazi 16
Grand Ayatollah Sayyid Abu al-Qasim al-Khu'i 20
Grand Ayatollah Sayyid 'Ali Sistani 22
'Allamah Sayyid Muhammad Husayn Tabataba'i 26
Ayatollah 'Abd al-Husayn Amini 28
Ayatollah Sayyid Muhammad Baqir Al-Sadr 30
Grand Ayatollah Muhammad Fadil Lankarani 32
Grand Ayatollah Husayn Nuri Hamadani 34
Grand Ayatollah Lutfullah Safi Golpaygani 36
Grand Ayatollah Husayn Wahid Khorasani 38
Grand Ayatollah Ja'far Subhani 42
Grand Ayatollah Bahjat 44
Grand Ayatollah Sayyid Musawi Shubayri Zanjani .. 48
Grand Ayatollah 'Abdullah Jawadi-Amuli 52
Grand Ayatollah Sayyid Mahmud Hashimi Shaherudi ... 54
Grand Ayatollah Muhammad Husayn Fadlullah 56
Grand Ayatollah Sayyid Muhammad Sa'id Hakim ... 58

Grand Ayatollah Bashir Najafi 62

Grand Ayatollah Shaykh Ishaq Fayyaz 66

Grand Ayatollah Qurban-'Ali Muhaqqiq Kabuli 70

Grand Ayatollah Sayyid Muhammad Shaherudi 72

Grand Ayatollah Sayyid Muhammad 'Ali Gurgani 74

Grand Ayatollah Husayn Mazaheri 78

Grand Ayatollah Sayyid Yusuf Madani Tabrizi 80

Grand Ayatollah Sayyid 'Abd Al-Karim Ardabili 82

Ayatollah Muhammad Taqi Misbah-Yazdi 84

Ayatollah Muhammad Rida Mahdawi Kani 86

Ayatollah Muhammad Yazdi 90

Ayatollah Asif Muhsini 94

Ayatollah Muhammad Mahdi Asifi 96

Ayatollah Muhammad 'Ali Taskhiri 100

Ayatollah Muhammad Hashimi Salihi 102

Ayatollah Murtada Mutahhari 104

In the Name of God, the Beneficent, the Merciful

Preface

This compilation of rulings by contemporary Shi'i scholars was first published in Farsi and Arabic as a response to the growing concern over *takfir*, or proclamations of excommunication of Muslims by other Muslims. These Shi'i scholars, who are at the upper echelon of Shi'i leadership and comprise the majority of the current and late twentieth-century *maraji'*, concur on the necessity of emphasising the concept of Muslim unity, regardless of sect, in Shi'i thought, and of promoting the importance of thoughtful social interactions between Muslims of varying sects in order to further a sense of genuine compassion and unity. This is all the more important in this day and age with the growing spectre of sectarian violence, particularly in regions ravaged by war. First published in 2015, it remains a current snapshot of the latest views of top Shi'i scholars.

We would like to extend our gratitude to Sheikh Ahmed Haneef for translating this work and Dr Amina Inloes for editing it.

The Islamic Centre of England
London, UK

Introduction

Today, apart from what its external enemies are doing, the divisiveness of extremism and takfirism (proclaiming Muslims as non-believers) has caused irreparable damage to Muslim society and the Islamic awakening. Not a day goes by without extremists hurling insults against what another *madhhab* (Islamic school of thought) holds in reverence. At the slightest excuse, the sullied hands of takfirists spill the innocent blood of Muslims and destroy the holy sites that have been etched in their identities. They are like the Kharijites, who in their misuse of the verses of the Holy Qur'an went on to kill and plunder Muslims; concerning the Kharijites, Imam 'Ali (A) said, "They used truth to promote falsehood." The puritanical attitude of the takfirists and extremists in their interpretation of religious teachings leads them to spill Muslim blood, seize their property and violate their honour. By inappropriately attributing some of these issues to the founders of *madhhab*s and inflating the untoward behaviours of some people, they stoke the fires of discord and disunity among Muslims and hurt their religious sentiments. The spread of a negative atmosphere and intra-Muslim strife are the results of these actions.

The *'ulama*, the *maraji' al-taqlid*, and followers of the School of the Ahl al-Bayt (A) maintain that insulting revered Islamic figures and proclaiming the followers of other sects as infidels are impermissible. Without hesitation, they have issued fatwas declaring these actions to be *haram* (forbidden). For this reason the Secretariat of the Congress on the Danger of Extremist and Takfirist Currents in cooperation with the Jurisdiction of the Representation of the Wali al-Faqih on Matters of Hajj and Ziyarat (Hawzeh-ye Namayandegi-ye Vali-ye Faqih dar Umur-e Hajj va Ziyarat) have resolved to publish the fatwas of Shi'i *maraji'* as an important step in the direction of strengthening the foundations for inter-*madhhab* convergence and bringing together as many of the *'ulama* and scholars of other *madhhab*s as possible to intellectually confront extremism and takfirism and their crimes.

This book comprises the religiously legal injunctions (*fatawa*) of grand *maraji' al-taqlid* and prominent Shi'i religious scholars concerning the legal prohibition (*hurmat*) – according to the Qur'an and the *hadith* – of insulting revered Islamic figures and calling the People of the Qiblah [Muslims] unbelievers. We hope that with the efforts and cooperation of all the *'ulama* in the world of Islam, we will witness the eradication of the strife of extremism and takfirism in the two spheres of thought and action from the Muslim world.

Head of Research
Secretariat of the Congress on the Danger of Extremist and Takfirist Currents

IMAM KHOMEINI

حضرت امام خمینی ﷺ

Muslim unity

We are one with Sunni Muslims. We are a unit, like a Muslim and his brother.

If someone says something that is divisive to Muslims, you should know that they are either ignorant or they would like to create discord between Muslims. It is not a Shi'i-Sunni issue. We are brothers, all of us.[1]

To all speakers and writers: whether in private or public, you have a *shar'i* religious obligation to avoid fomenting discord and division in your discourse and writing, even as hints or allusions. This is because today division is a deadly poison for the Muslim *ummah*. You should know that in the present environment fomenting division is nothing but following the *nafs al-ammarah* (the soul that commands to evil) or the inner devil and serving the superpowers – in particular, globally rapacious America. It is also a major sin through which Satan lets the name of Islam flow off tongues and pens. They should know that the Islamic Revolution will not tolerate this and will punish those guilty of this.[2]

In Islam there is no Shi'i-Sunni division at all, and there should not be any division between Shi'is and Sunnis. We should maintain a united voice. Our Imams advised us to keep our communities together, and whoever wants to cause strife is either ignorant or malicious.[3]

---

[1] Imam Khomeini, *Sahifeh-ye Nur*, vol. 5, p. 77.
[2] Ibid., vol. 14, p. 157.
[3] Ibid., vol. 5, p. 38.

Grand Ayatollah Sayyid 'Ali Khamene'i

آیت الله العظمی سید علی خامنه‌ای دامظله

Question

What are the compelling reasons and clear sources of Muslim unity under the current conditions? What is the opinion of your excellence concerning the use of the term "Islamic *ummah*" as applied to those who adhere to Islamic beliefs like the four Sunni sects or other sects like the Zaydis, the Zahiris, or Ibadis that believe in the fundamental principles of the religion of Islam? Is it permissible or not to takfirise them? What are the limits of doing *takfir*, and what are the parameters today?

We pray to Almighty God for your success and long life in your service to Islam and Muslims, in particular, the Shi'i world.

Answer

Every Islamic sect is considered part of the Muslim *ummah* and is entitled to all Islamic privileges. Sowing seeds of division among Islamic schools of thought goes against the Holy Qur'an and the Sunnah of the Noble Prophet of Islam (S). Additionally, it weakens the Muslims and makes them vulnerable to their enemies. Therefore, accusing the Islamic sects above of unbelief or *takfir* is not allowed under any circumstance.[4]

---

[4] Ghazi ibn Muhammad ibn Talal, *Ijma' al-Muslimin 'ala Ihtiram Madhahib al-Din*, p. 214.

His fatwa on the impermissibility of insulting figures revered by Sunnis

In answer to the request for a fatwa by a number of *'ulama* and Shi'a scholars from Ahsa, Saudi Arabia concerning the issue of insulting the wife of the Prophet of Islam (S), the Leader of the Islamic Revolution said: "Insulting the symbols and revered personalities of our brothers among the Ahl al-Sunnah is *haram*. It is even more so *haram* to impugn the honour of or disrespect the wife of the Holy Prophet (S). When this type of behaviour is not allowed regarding the wives of the prophets in general, it would be especially so with respect to the chief among them, the honourable Messenger of Allah (S)."

The Shaykh al-Azhar of Egypt commends Ayatollah Khamene'i's fatwa

Dr Ahmad al-Tayyib, the Shaykh al-Azhar, declared in a statement that this fatwa was issued at a crucial time to prevent a split and estrangement between the two schools [Sunnis and Shi'is]. Shaykh Ahmad al-Tayyib continued:

I was very impressed and happy by this holy fatwa of the Honourable Imam 'Ali Khamene'i concerning insulting the Companions (R) or being offensive towards the wives of the Holy Prophet (S). This fatwa was issued with correct knowledge and deep comprehension in response to the danger of what the creators of strife were doing. It is also a statement of desire and yearning for Muslim unity. Another thing that adds importance to this fatwa is that someone who is a great Muslim *'alim*, who is a grand *marja'* of the Shi'is, and is the Supreme Leader of the Islamic Republic of Iran has issued such a fatwa.⁵

Further statements

Every statement and action that would inflame the fires of division among Muslims, insult the revered holy figures of any Muslim community, or make *takfir* on any Muslim sect is serving the camp of unbelief and polytheism is betraying Islam, and from the point of view of the *shari'ah* it is *haram*.⁶

Both Sunnis that collaborate with America and Shi'is that are exported from London to the world are brothers of Satan and agents of Western supremacism.⁷

The enemy threatens the very existence of Islam, and every community and school of thought should stand together and form a united fist and not let the enemy infiltrate the vast territory of the Muslim world.⁸

I swear by Allah! Those who go among the Shi'is and put hatred and malice in their hearts against Sunnis, and those who go among Sunnis and put hatred and malice into their hearts against Shi'is like neither Shi'is nor Sunnis. They do not like Islam, but of course they do not know it. Many of them do not understand.

Because of ignorance and forgetfulness or to purposefully incite division, some Shi'is insult the revered figures of the Ahl al-Sunnah.

---

⁵ As mentioned on the Al-Manar television channel; see <http://www.shia12.net>.
⁶ Message to the Great Hajj Congress. Aban 1392 (*hijri* solar calendar). Official Centre for the Safeguarding and Publishing the Works of Ayatollah Sayyid Ali Khamene'i <http://farsi.khamenei.ir/message-content?id=24203>.
⁷ Remarks at commemorations of the 25ᵗʰ anniversary of the passing of Imam Khomeini, 14/3/1394 (*hijri* solar calendar).
⁸ Ibid.

I would like to state that the conduct of the two groups is forbidden in religious law (*haram shar'i*) and is against the law.[9]

Sometimes someone helps a Shi'i defeat a Sunni, and sometimes someone helps a Sunni defeat a Shi'i. The enemy wants this. When divisions take place, when sectarianism appears, when mistrust happens between each other, when we see each other as traitors, it is natural for us not to co-operate with each other. And if we did co-operate, we would not be sincere with each other. This is the very thing the enemy is after. Both the Shi'i religious scholar and the Sunni religious scholar should know this. It is evident that both schools of thought have some differences in their doctrines (*usul*) and their religious practices (*furu*), but they are not differences that should bring about enmity. One should never imagine that the Ahl al-Bayt of the Prophet (S) is exclusive to the Shi'is and belongs to them. Not at all! They belong to the entire world of Islam. Who wouldn't accept Fatima al Zahra (A)? Who would not accept Husayn (A), one of the chiefs of the youths of Paradise? Who would not accept the great Imams of the Shi'is?[10]

---

[9] Remarks to the gathering of the people of Kurdistan Province, 23/2/1388 (*hijri* solar calendar).

[10] On a visit by Shi'i and Sunni religious scholars and seminary students from Kurdistan, 23/2/1388 (*hijri* solar calendar).

Grand Ayatollah Nasir Makarim Shirazi

آیت الله العظمی ناصر مکارم شیرازی دامظله

Muslim unity

I have stated many times that Muslim unity and bringing Islamic schools of thought together are the most important issues at all times but especially under the present conditions. Therefore, all types of insults against the revered figures of the other schools of thought are not permissible. All Muslims, not just Shi'is and Sunnis, should be careful that we do not fall into the snare of the enemy of Islam and create sectarian strife. Committing suicide attacks and spilling innocent blood are among the worst of mortal sins and clear instances of committing corruption on the earth,[11] and could warrant everlasting torment in the fires of Hell. It changes the face of Islam from one where mercy and kindness are its standards to one identified with harshness and offensiveness. May God guide all those who have made errors and committed sins.

Insulting the revered figures of the Muslims is *haram*, and we should show respect to the revered figures of the Sunnis. If someone shows irreverence to the revered figures of the Sunnis, this has nothing to do with Shi'is. Love for the Ahl al-Bayt (A) is not exclusive to Shi'is; all Islamic schools of thought love the Ahl al-Bayt (A). Throughout history, the actions of the aggrandizers have been to create schisms in the Islamic world through devilish policies and weaken the economic, cultural and political resources of Islamic countries to gain domination over them. We should therefore confront the enemy with solidarity and unity.[12]

---

[11] A reference to Quran 2:11.
[12] Remarks by Grand Ayatollah Makarim Shirazi on a visit by Shi'i and Sunni *'ulama* from Turbat-e Jam, 21/5/1394 (*hijri* solar calendar).

The common aspects shared by Muslims are much more than their differences. For this very reason, we should concentrate on what we have in common and come closer to forging unity between us. Activities that would result in loss of the trust that Muslims have for each other should not be allowed to take place. Shi'is should not insult the revered figures of other schools of thought because it will cause internal conflict. There is no problem speaking about Mawla 'Ali (A), but one should not insult others. I hope and pray that God incapacitates all those that attempt to cause schism and discord among Muslims.[13]

The issue of Muslim unity is of supreme importance. I announced in my fatwa that we do not give permission for even the slightest insult against the revered figures of another school of thought – regardless of what the dispute may be – that causes fighting and conflict between Muslims. It should be noted that things about which we disagree are not to the extent that they should cause conflict. The theological principles of the various schools of thought are one, and we should focus upon them so that disputes do not arise. The Holy Qur'an states that those who incite schism are outside the pale of monotheism. Let us preserve security through unity.[14]

---

[13] Remarks at the commencement of advanced studies in jurisprudence (*dars-e kharij-e fiqh*), 25 Dey 1392 (*hijri* solar calendar).
[14] Remarks on the visit of a number of Sunni *'ulama* from Kurdistan Province, 2/9/1394 (*hijri* solar calendar).

Grand Ayatollah Sayyid Abu al-Qasim al-Khu'i

آيت الله العظمى سيد ابوالقاسم خوبى ﷾

Statements

The things that contribute to ascertaining Islam are as follows: belief in the oneness of God, prophecy, and the return to God. These result in (those who affirm these beliefs) being accepted as *tahir* (pure) and entitles them to respect for their rights to property and life as well as other rights. All sects of Islam believe in them.[15]

It is commonly known that Twelver Shi'is hold that other Muslims are ritually pure, even if they hold disagreeing views or are members of differing sects.[16] As long as the *shahadatayn* is still verbally made [even] by one who denies the *wilayah* of the Imams, that person is considered to be a Muslim. Such was the unequivocal way of the Imams of the Ahl al-Bayt (A); this substantiates them being considered ritually pure as well as Muslim.[17]

The ruling on the Zaydis, Ismailis, and others is like the ruling on the Sunnis concerning their being considered ritually pure and Muslim.[18]

---

[15] Ayatollah al-Khu'i, *al-Tanqih*, vol. 2, p. 62.
[16] Ibid., p. 83.
[17] Ibid., p. 85.
[18] Ibid.

Grand Ayatollah Sayyid 'Ali Sistani

آیت‌الله العظمی سیدعلی سیستانی دامظله

Question

We have a request for you to guide millions of Muslims on this particular subject. Is anyone who says the *shahadatayn*, turns towards the *qiblah*, prays the *salah*, and follows one of the eight schools of thought (Hanafi, Shafi'i, Maliki, Hanbali, Ja'fari, Zaydi, Ibadi, or Zahiri) counted as Muslim with their lives, honour, and property being inviolable?

Answer

Firstly, anyone who utters the *shahadatayn*, does not contradict it in their speech and does not hold enmity and hostility towards the Ahl al-Bayt (A) is considered a Muslim.[19]

Secondly, from the viewpoint of the Shi'is, the Ahl al-Sunnah are counted as Muslims, and all of the laws of Islam apply to them. Marrying them is permissible. They can inherit from Shi'is, and Shi'is can inherit from them. The lives property and honour of all of them are inviolable. Statements that claim that Shi'is consider those who fought in the Battle of Badr [with the Prophet (S)], those [who took the pact of] Bay'at al-Ridwan [with the Prophet (S)], the believing Emigrants and Helpers, and the leaders of the Islamic schools of thought and their followers are unbelievers are pure lies.

Cursing the revered figures of the Ahl al-Sunnah is contrary to the teachings the Ahl al-Bayt imparted to their Shi'is and their students.[20]

---

[19] Ghazi ibn Muhammad ibn Talal, *Ijma' al-Muslimin 'ala Ihtiram Madhahib al-Din*, p. 220.
[20] See <http://www.teribon.ir/archives/235252>.

I love everyone. The religion of Islam is the religion of love, and I am surprised at how (our) enemies could create a schism between our schools of thought. Shi'is should defend the social and political rights of the Ahl al-Sunnah before they defend their own rights. Our discourse should be an invitation to unity. Just as I said before, I am saying now that you should not say "The Sunnis are our brothers"; rather you should say, "Sunnis are our life". I listen to the sermons of the Sunni imams of the Friday prayers more often than the sermons of the Shi'is. We don't believe in differences between Arabs and Kurds. Islam brings all of us together. In researching Islamic law, I used to cite the *fatawa* of the Ahl al-Sunnah. We are united in our Ka'bah, *salat*, and fasting.[21]

---

[21] Message by Grand Ayatollah Sistani to the first Congress of Shi'i and Sunni Ulama, 3 November 2007.

'ALLAMAH SAYYID MUHAMMAD HUSAYN TABATABA'I

علامه سید محمد حسین طباطبایی ﷺ

The early period of Islam

The Shi'is in the early period of Islam never set themselves apart from the ranks of the majority. They strove together with the wider Muslim population and offered their advice. Right now, every Muslim should keep in mind our common agreement on the fundamental sacred principles of Islam. Amidst all the pressure and discontent brought upon them by foreigners and their external agents throughout this whole time, Muslims should come to their senses, leave aside sectarian behaviour and form themselves into one rank.[22]

---

[22] See <http://www.tasnimnews.com/fa/news/1393/10/20/609930>.

AYATOLLAH ʿABD AL-HUSAYN AMINI

آیت الله عبدالحسین امینی﷿

Diversity

The beliefs and opinions of schools of thought in Islam vary. However, the roots of brotherhood – [which are] that the Quran so clearly says "the believers are brethren" (49:10) – will never be excised, no matter how high the intellectual wrangle and the theological and sect-oriented squabble might be. This was the way of the *salaf* (pious predecessors), especially the Companions and their successors.[23]

We writers [come] from different regions and environments in the world. With all the differences we might have in our theological principles and religious practice, we have one common aspect, and that is that we believe in God and the Prophet of God (S). In the body of each and every one of us, let us have one spirit, one sentiment, and that is the spirit of Islam and sincerity in speech.[24]

---

[23] Ayatollah Amini, *al-Ghadir*, vol. 5, Introduction (under the heading 'Nazariyyah Karimah').
[24] Ibid.

Ayatollah Sayyid Muhammad Baqir Al-Sadr

آیت ‌الله شهید سید محمد باقر صدرﷻ

The flag of Islam

I have spent all of my life promoting unity and brotherhood between Shi'is and Sunnis. I have defended and supported all of their messages conducive to unity and every belief that they have embraced. I am a brother and son of the Sunnis to the same extent that I am a brother and son of Shi'is.[25]

From the time I knew myself and discovered my responsibility within the community I have endeavoured to bring Shia'is together with the Sunni Arabs and Kurds. I would stand up to defend and support every message that could bring them together, and every belief that would bring them closer and of one accord. With all my thought and my being, I have lived completely for Islam, the very Islam that is the Path of Salvation and the goal of all.[26]

Half a century ago, Shi'i *ulama* grasped the flag of Islam and issued *fatawa* of jihad to help Sunni sovereignties. Hundreds of thousands of Shi'is went to war and were unstinting as their blood soaked the ground; this was to protect the flag of Islam by supporting a Sunni government which was standing for Islam[27]

---

[25] Sayyid Kazim Ha'iri, *Mabahith al-Usul*, vol. 1, pp. 151-153.
[26] Ibid., p. 151.
[27] Ibid., p. 152.

Grand Ayatollah Muhammad Fadil Lankarani

آیت‌الله‌العظمی محمد فاضل لنکرانی ﷺ

Question

Accepting that there are incontrovertible and clear reasons for the necessity of Muslim unity under the current conditions, what is your Excellency's opinion on the use of the term 'Islamic *ummah*' for the followers of Islamic sects such as: the four sects of the Ahl al-Sunnah, and others such as the Zaydis, the Zahiris, or the Ibadis, all of whom believe in the principles of the religion of Islam?

Is it permissible or not to denounce them as unbelievers (*takfir*)? What are the limitations and criteria that should govern practicing *takfir* at the present time? We pray to Almighty God for your Excellency's success, and a long life in the service of Islam and Muslims especially in the Shi'i world.

Answer

As long as they do not deny the principles and necessary aspects of the clear religion of Islam or, God forbid, insult the pure Imams, all of these sects are considered sects of Islam.[28]

---

[28] Ghazi ibn Muhammad ibn Talal, *Ijma' al-Muslimin 'ala Ihtiram Madhahib al-Din*, pp. 245-256.

GRAND AYATOLLAH HUSAYN NURI HAMADANI

آیت الله العظمی حسین نوری همدانی دامﻅله

Muslim unity

Islam says that Sunnis and Shi'is are brothers, and they should not fall into disagreement and make it open because the enemy will misuse it. The more our interrelationships increase, the better it is for Islam because we have a common enemy, and they are against the principles of Islam. We are all brothers and we should act in unison. If we just stand aside and watch on this field of battle, the enemy will swallow us. The Qur'an sees us all as brothers, and brotherhood is one of the most intense types of relationships between two people which the Qur'an emphasises. The Ahl al-Bayt (A) advised Shi'is to interact with Sunnis, to attend their mosques and pray behind them, and they even said that the reward of such a prayer is the like of praying behind the Prophet (S). In the past Sunnis and Shi'is studied in the same *madrasah*.[29]

---

[29] On the occasion of a visit by Sunni party members of the Islamic Consultative Council, 15/10/1393 (*hijri* solar calendar).

Grand Ayatollah Lutfullah Safi Golpaygani

آیت الله العظمی لطف الله صافی گلپایگانی دامظله

The true face of Islam

Whoever testifies to the oneness of Almighty God verbally and to the messengership of the Seal of the Prophets, Muhammad ibn 'Abdullah (S), is a Muslim. His life, reputation and property are inviolable, and no one has the right to insult their revered religious figures. Carrying out suicide attacks and spilling Muslim blood is a major sin.

Muslims have a responsibility to show the world the true face of Islam as a religion of mercy, love and kindness. We should all stand united in one rank to promote our beloved Islam and guide people in all corners of the globe and through unity and togetherness eliminate the treacherous designs of the enemies of the Qur'an.

إِنْ تَنْصُرُوا اللَّهَ يَنْصُرْكُمْ وَيُثَبِّتْ أَقْدَامَكُمْ

If you support Allah, Allah will support you and make your stance firm. (Qur'an 47:7)

GRAND AYATOLLAH HUSAYN WAHID KHORASANI

آیت الله العظمی حسین وحید خراسانی دامظله

Question

We are a community living in a Sunni area. They think we are *kafir*s and say that we are *kafir*s. Under these circumstances, is it also possible for us to treat them in like manner and, just as they take us to be *kafir*s, we do the same to them? We request that you inform us regarding our *shar'i* responsibility while facing these attacks.

Answer

Anyone who verbally bears witness to the oneness of God Almighty and the messengership of the Seal of the Prophets (S) is a Muslim and his life, his honour and his property are inviolable just like the life, the honour and the property of one who follows the Ja'fari school of thought. Your legal responsibility is that you treat kindly those who have said the *shahadatayn* even if they consider you an unbeliever. Have good social relations with them. If, they treat you unjustly, you should not deviate from the straight path of truth and justice. If one of them becomes sick, and visit him. If one of them passes away, attend his funeral. If they have a need that they request from you, then fulfil it. Comply with God's decree when He says:

وَلَا يَجْرِمَنَّكُمْ شَنَآنُ قَوْمٍ عَلَى أَلَّا تَعْدِلُوا اعْدِلُوا هُوَ أَقْرَبُ لِلتَّقْوَى

Ill feeling for a people should not lead you – because they barred you from entering the Sacred Mosque – to transgress. Cooperate in piety and Godwariness, but do not cooperate in sin and aggression, and be wary of Allah. (Qur'an 5:2)

And act on God's orders when He says:

وَلَا تَقُولُوا لِمَنْ أَلْقَى إِلَيْكُمُ السَّلَامَ لَسْتَ مُؤْمِناً

Do not say to someone who offers you peace, "You are not a believer." (Quran 4:94)[30]

Indeed, understanding in these matters has disappeared. This type of behaviour leads to the shedding of innocent blood which the exhortations of the Imams (A) are against. Open curses and insults are not permissible. First of all, open cursing in general is forbidden, and this is stressed in the commands of the religion. Secondly authentic narrations say, 'Pray in their mosques'. Visit their sick. Attend their funerals. The narrations say, 'Be an adornment to us, and do not be a disgrace to us.' In these narrations two points arise; one is negative and the other is positive. The negative point – which is 'do not be a disgrace to us' – is that you should not harbour enmity towards the revered figures of another school of thought. Do not insult their revered figures; cursing and insulting their great figures is not permissible because it can alienate them from the Ahl al-Bayt (A) and their teachings. The positive aspect – which says 'be an adornment to us' – tells us that we should attend their Friday Prayers, that we should show them love, visit their sick, and set forth our speeches and teachings to them; the main point here is spreading the teachings of the Ahl al-Bayt (A). This is a path that we have not been versed in – the path of positivity.[31]

---

[30] See 'Hosn-i mu'ashirat ba mokhalifin-e madhhab', in the Official Website of the Office of Grand Ayatollah Wahid Khorasani, Aban 1387 (*hijri* solar calendar) <http://wahidkhorasani.com>.

[31] Remarks by Grand Ayatollah Wahid Khorasani on the visit of Ayatollah Muhsin Araki, General Secretary of the World Assembly for Convergence of Islamic Schools of Thought on the 2nd Khordad 1393 <http://taghribnews.com/vdchzwnz623nm-d.tft2.html>.

GRAND AYATOLLAH JA'FAR SUBHANI

آیت الله العظمی جعفر سبحانی دامظله

The Book of God

All Muslims should take the Book of God as their model. They should be united and avoid any type of activity that would cause division especially at this time when the unbelievers and the forces of arrogance are plotting to cause division between Muslims and spilling their blood at each other's hands.

When Imam Ash'ari was on his deathbed, he called all his students around him and said, "Bear witness that I never did *takfir* upon any of the People of the Qiblah [Muslims] because all of them have one object of worship, and all of them are under the flag of Islam."

What we have said makes it incumbent upon us to respect the sentiments and beliefs of others and not to relate to them in a way that leads to division. The levelling of insults at the Companions, which the Shi'is have been accused of, is an unjust act that is totally wrong. Shi'is should dissociate themselves from this type of activity. They should see the Companions as examples, as Imam 'Ali ibn Husayn (A) said in the following prayer:

اللهم وأصحاب محمّد خاصة، الذين أحسنوا الصحبة والذين أبلوا البلاء الحسن في نصره وكانفوه وأسرعوا إلى وفادته وسابقوا إلى دعوته

O Allah! And as for the Companions of Muhammad specifically, [bless] those who did well in companionship, who stood the good test in helping him, responded to him, assisted him, hastened to receive him in kindness and strove to respond to his call.[32]

---

[32] The prayer is from Imam Zayn al-'Abidin, *al-Sahifah al-Sajjadiyah*, supplication 4 (for the Companions that supported the Prophet (S)). Excerpt is from the message of Grand Ayatollah Ja'far Subhani to the hajj pilgrims.

GRAND AYATOLLAH BAHJAT

آیت الله العظمی بهجت ﷫

Brotherhood

We should let the people know that we have amity with the Ahl al-Sunnah. We have no problems with them. They are following their own *tariqah* (spiritual path), and we are following our own. We have our evidence, but that is beside the point. They also acknowledge the two testimonies of faith (*shahadatayn*) which we acknowledge. Based upon this we have no difference with Sunnis apart from the superfluous actions that they do. You say that every year strangers come to Shi'a neighbourhoods in Baghdad and, in the morning, cry out 'prayer is better than sleep (*al-salat khairun min al-nawm*).' In Sunni neighbourhoods also, someone comes and recites in the in the call to prayer 'hasten to the best of deeds (*hayya 'ala khayr al-'amal*)'.[33] The Sunnis say that these are Shi'is who have come to undermine the Sunnis, and vice versa. Then they both start to fight until the foreigners make themselves rich as brokers of peace.[34]

Why couldn't we have come together and agreed to be united – brothers, in one accord? Unity is a matter so self-evident that even non-religious people and non-believers subscribe to it[35].

Shi'i-Sunni conflict is a matter of colonialism. The most important matter is that the two sects have a love for the Ahl al-Bayt (A) [36]

---

[33] The former is part of the Sunni call to morning prayer, and the latter is part of the Shi'i call to morning prayer.
[34] Centre for the Collation and Publication of the Works of Grand Ayatollah Bahjat <http://bahjat.ir/fa/content/5698>.
[35] *Dar Mahdar-e Bahjat*, vol. 1, p. 186.
[36] Mohammad Mohammadi Ray Shahri, *Zamzam-e 'Erfan (Yadnameh-ye Faqih-e 'Aref-e Hadrat Ayatollah Mohammad Taqi Bahjat)*, p. 292.

Whoever does not desire Muslim unity is not a Muslim. Our Imams prayed along with them in their congregational prayers in the name of Muslim unity.[37]

---

[37] Ibid.

GRAND AYATOLLAH SAYYID MUSAWI SHUBAYRI ZANJANI

آیت الله العظمی سید موسی شبیری زنجانی دامﻈله

Muslim solidarity

Whoever says the *shahadatayn* verbally (unless he is a Nasibi or a Kharijite) is a Muslim, and the rulings of Islam in such areas like the permissibility to marry, to inherit mutually, and to show respect for his life, property, and so on apply to him. Those who foment sectarianism amidst the ranks of Islam and pronounce *takfir* upon other Islamic sects are outside the reality of Islam. Even though they might not be direct agents of colonialism, they are, without doubt, furthering the corrupt aims of the colonialists who aim to undermine the principles of Islam, destroy the religion of the Noble Prophet of Islam (S) and render forgotten His Sublime Name. Suicide attacks by these groups only serve to please the unbelievers and those enemies who swear that they are aiding Islam.

الَّذِينَ ضَلَّ سَعْيُهُمْ فِى الْحَيَاةِ الدُّنْيَا وَ هُمْ يَحْسَبُونَ أَنَّهُمْ يُحْسِنُونَ صُنْعاً قُلْ هَلْ نُنَبِّئُكُمْ بِالْأَخْسَرِينَ أَعْمَالاً

Shall We tell you of those who have lost out the most on their deeds? It is they whose efforts strayed in the life of this world, while they reckoned that they were doing good. (Qur'an 18:103-104)

God willing, all Muslims will become aware of the deceptions of the enemies of Islam, take a firm position and persist in their endeavours in establishing the greatness and honour of Islam.

It is necessary for all Muslims, whether Shi'i or Sunni, to promote solidarity with all of their vigilance and speak with one voice. They should adopt appropriate conduct when confronting these groups and avoid all forms of conflict and sectarianism.[38]

---

[38] Official media headquarters of the office of Grand Ayatollah Shubayri Zanjani <http://zanjani.net/index.aspx?pid=99&articleid=63309>.

Grand Ayatollah 'Abdullah Jawadi-Amuli

آیت الله العظمی عبدالله جوادی آملی دامظله

Respecting revered figures

Every nation has revered figures which they respect, and this is in no way particular to monotheism or atheism. One must avoid insulting or treating them disrespectfully. For this reason, the Noble Qur'an says concerning this:

وَ لا تَسُبُّوا الَّذِينَ يدْعُونَ مِنْ دُونِ اللهِ فَيَسُبُّوا اللَّهَ عَدْواً بِغَيرِ عِلْمٍ كَذلِكَ زَينَّا لِكُلِّ أُمَّةٍ عَمَلَهُمْ ثُمَّ إلى رَبِّهِمْ مَرْجِعُهُمْ فَينَبِّئُهُمْ بِما كانُوا يعْمَلُونَ

> Do not insult those they invoke other than Allah, lest they insult Allah in enmity without knowledge. Thus We have made pleasing to every community their deeds. Then to their Lord is their return, and He will inform them about what they used to do. (Qur'an 6:108)

No one has the right to insult revered figures because they might turn around, and God forbid, speak ill of the revered figures of the believers.

Insulting the Companions, disrespecting revered figures of Shi'is and Sunnis, and insulting and wrongfully belittling the beliefs of either group are forbidden (*haram*). They create conflict and ignite the flames of sectarianism and discord and destroy the basis of unity of the Muslim *ummah*. This is a major sin that everyone should seriously refrain from doing.[39]

---

[39] Message of Grand Ayatollah Jawadi Amuli to the hajj pilgrims in 1392 (*hijri* solar calendar).

Grand Ayatollah Sayyid Mahmud Hashimi Shaherudi

آیت‌الله‌العظمی سید محمود هاشمی شاهرودی دامظله

Respecting revered figures

Magnifying differences and creating barriers with other Islamic schools of thought are against *shari'ah* law. The enemy would exploit this as negative propaganda to exacerbate these differences.

The enemy exploits differences between schools of thought and communities; they exacerbate them to influence the community. They are always trying to split the Muslim world through differences in theology and jurisprudence. We should be careful of people who draw sectarian lines and amplify our differences, while at the same time we should respect each other's jurisprudential opinions. If we want to draw sectarian lines, we should have hundreds of lines in our own Shi'i community because every *mujtahid* in the Shi'i *madhhab* has a particular opinion. Every form of insult towards the followers of a *madhhab* is *haram*. Any type of belittling a belief is wrong, and *'ulama* should also make it *haram* so that it would be recognised in our penal code as a crime and be tackled as such.

Insulting the revered figures of the Ahl al-Sunnah is contrary to the way of the Ahl al-Bayt (A). The Imams (A) never insulted the revered figures of Ahl al-Sunnah, not to mention the wife of the Prophet (S). We should avail ourselves of what the Prophet and Imams said and how they lived. The Imams never cursed or insulted revered figures, and therefore we should not do this.[40]

---

[40] Speech by Grand Ayatollah Sayyid Mahmud Hashimi Shaherudi on 21/04/1393 to a gathering of judicial councils based in Mazandaran.

GRAND AYATOLLAH MUHAMMAD HUSAYN FADLULLAH

آیت‌الله‌العظمی سید محمّد حسین فضل الله ﷺ

The *ummah*

Islam is the verbal expression of the *shahadatayn* along with belief in the necessary concomitants [to the *shahadatayn*] that are mentioned in the Qur'an. Thus whoever finds these necessary concomitants incumbent upon him is a Muslim, and all of the laws of Islam apply to him. This is so unless that person denies an essential aspect of the religion of Islam, and he recognises the concomitant of that denial, which is that this denial leads to giving the lie to the Messenger of God (S). However, differences in speculative matters that *'ulama* disagree over do not result in *takfir*.[41]

We believe that the followers of all the schools of thought in Islam are members of the Islamic *ummah* and doing *takfir* of the Muslim *ummah*, in whatever form it may be, is not permissible. In cases where there is disagreement, it should be dealt with by rational discussion on the relevant issue, as the Qur'an has said:

فان تنازعتم فى شىء فردوه الى الله و الرسول

And if you disagree about anything, return it to Allah and his Messenger. (Qur'an 4:59)[42]

---

[41] Ghazi ibn Muhammad ibn Talal, Ijma' al-Muslimin 'ala Ihtiram Madhahib al-Din, p. 255.
[42] Ibid.

Grand Ayatollah Sayyid Muhammad Sa'id Hakim

آیت‌الله العظمی سیدمحمدسعید حکیم دامظله

Question

Please guide the millions of Muslims regarding this particularly important subject: is someone who utters the *shahadatayn*, prays facing the *qiblah*, and adheres to one of the eight schools of thought (Hanafi, Shafi'i, Maliki, Hanbali, Ja'fari, Zaydi, Ibadi, or Zahiri) considered a Muslim with his life, honour and property inviolable?

Answer

Doing *takfir* upon the Companions and Muslims of whatever other school of thought is not something Shi'is believe in. This belief of ours arises from the spirit of Islam and its principles. This point is understood from a number of narrations by the Shi'i Imams (A) on the subject, and in the legal judgements (*fatawa*) of jurisprudents.[43]

Question

Many Muslims and non-Muslims ask us about Islamic unity and connections between the different Islamic schools of thought. We would like your Excellency to answer the following questions:

1) Is someone who follows the Hanafi, Maliki, Shafi'i, Hanbali, Ja'fari, Zaydi, or Ibadi school of thought considered a Muslim?
2) What are the limits of doing *takfir* in Islam? Is it permissible for a Muslim to do *takfir* upon the followers of one of the well-known schools of thought mentioned in the question above,

---

[43] Sayyid Muhammad Sa'id Hakim, *Fi Rihab al-'Aqidah*, vol. 1, pp. 34-43.

or the Ash'arite or Mu'tazilite schools? Is pronouncing *takfir* upon followers of Sufism permissible?

Answer

1) Confessing the *shahadatayn* verbally and performing the obligatory actions and necessary elements that are binding in religion, such as canonical prayer, that would make us say that someone is a Muslim is sufficient [to be considered a Muslim].
2) The answer can be found in what was said before this.[44]

---

[44] Ghazi ibn Muhammad ibn Talal, Ijma' al-Muslimin 'ala Ihtiram Madhahib al-Din, p. 225.

GRAND AYATOLLAH BASHIR NAJAFI

آیت الله العظمی بشیر نجفی دامظلہ

Question

Many Muslims and non-Muslims ask us about Islamic unity and connections between the different Islamic schools of thought. We would like your Excellency to answer the following questions:

1) Is someone who follows the Hanafi, Maliki, Shafi'i, Hanbali, Ja'fari, Zaydi, or Ibadi schools of thought considered a Muslim?
2) What are the limits of doing *takfir* in Islam? Is it permissible for a Muslim to do *takfir* upon the followers of one of the well-known schools of thought mentioned in the question above, or the Ash'arite or Mu'tazilite schools? Is pronouncing *takfir* upon followers of Sufism permissible?

Answer

1) Whosoever confesses to the oneness of God and the messengership of Muhammad ibn 'Abdullah (S) verbally and believes that messengership and Prophethood end with him, and who also believes in the eschatology that comes with the faith, while not denying any of the above and is firm in his Muslim identity, is counted as a Muslim. He falls under all of the laws of Islam and as such, his life, property and honour are inviolable. It is also obligatory on all Muslims to defend his property and his honour. And Allah knows best.
2) It is not permissible to pronounce *takfir* on anyone who utters the *shahadatayn* verbally – i.e. bearing witness to the oneness of God and bearing witness to the prophethood Muhammad

ibn 'Abdullah (S) – ad believes in the Day of Judgment and does not deny any of those matters that a Muslim would affirm. There are also narrations from the Prophet (S) forbidding that. Anyone who exacerbates sectarianism between schools of thought or pronounces *takfir* on one of the schools of thought mentioned above is ignorant and is displaying ignorance, or is an enemy of Islam that has infiltrated [the community] with the aim of inciting sectarianism and creating rifts among the Muslims in service of supremacist unbelievers. And Allah knows best.[45]

---

[45] Ghazi ibn Muhammad ibn Talal, Ijma' al-Muslimin 'ala Ihtiram Madhahib al-Din, pp. 235-237.

GRAND AYATOLLAH SHAYKH ISHAQ FAYYAZ

آیت‌الله‌العظمی شیخ اسحاق فیاض دامت‌ظله

Question

Is someone who follows the Hanafi, Shafi'i, Hanbali, Maliki, Ja'fari, Zaydi, or Ibadi school of thought a Muslim?

Answer

[Followers of] all of the schools of thought of Islam are Muslims. The criterion for being Muslim is bearing witness to the oneness of Almighty God and bearing witness to the messengership of the Prophet (S). Whosoever says in Arabic, 'I bear witness that there is no god but Allah and I bear witness that Muhammad is the Messenger of Allah' is a Muslim and will be covered by all of the laws of Islam making his life, his honour and his property inviolable. This is the case whether the person is someone following the Ja'fari school of thought, the Zaydi [school], or the Sunni [schools]; whatever the school of thought might be, whether it be Hanafi, Shafi'i, Maliki, Hanbali, Ibadi, and so on.[46]

Question

What are the limits on *takfir* in Islam? Can one pronounce *takfir* on a Muslim who follows one of the well-known schools of thought in Islam or hold Ash'arite or Mu'tazilite beliefs? Is it permissible to pronounce *takfir* upon those who follow genuine Sufi *tariqah*s?

---

[46] Ibid., p. 229.

Answer

The criterion for unbelief (*kufr*) is denying divine oneness and the messengership. Therefore, pronouncing *takfir* upon the followers of Ash'arite doctrines, the Mu'tazilites, or followers of Sufi *tariqah*s is not permissible. This is because they acknowledge divine oneness and messengership. For this reason, from the time of the Imams (A) until the present, we cannot find from among the great *'ulama* anyone who had pronounced *takfir* upon the followers of the other schools of thought.[47]

---

[47] Ibid. pp. 229-231.

GRAND AYATOLLAH QURBAN-'ALI MUHAQQIQ KABULI

آیت الله العظمی قربانعلی محقق کابلی دامظله

Respecting revered figures

Restrain yourself from being disrespectful towards the revered figures of the Ahl al-Sunnah. Today, more than at any other time, the world of Islam is confronted by [difficult] circumstances. In this situation, one feels the necessity of unity and solidarity with the *ummah* despite our differences in nationality and race, and jurisprudential and *madhhabi* disagreements with each other. In the meantime, the scheming enemy and ignorant friends, unfamiliar with the basic principles of the clear religion of Islam, are like the two blades of a pair of scissors that threaten to cut the manifest rope, which is the unity and brotherhood of Muslims.[48]

In this period of time, the published legal opinions (*risalat*) of Islamic scholars struggle with communal extremism, nationalism and sectarianism that form the main roots of hypocrisy in the Muslim community.[49]

---

[48] Remarks by his Eminence concerning stirring up divisiveness. Ahlulbayt Channel, Shawwal 1431 AH. See the official website for Grand Ayatollah Muhaqqiq Kabuli <http://www.mohaqeq.org/fa/news/40.html>.

[49] Message of Grand Ayatollah Muhaqqiq Kabuli to the symposium on the thought of Shahid Ayatollah Wa'iz Behsudi
<http://afghanistan.shafaqna.com/topic/item/49655>.

GRAND AYATOLLAH SAYYID MUHAMMAD HUSAYNI SHAHERUDI

آیت الله العظمی سید محمد حسینی شاهرودی دامظله

The dignity of believers

Anyone who testifies to the sentence 'there is no god but Allah and Muhammad (S) is the Messenger of Allah' is a Muslim, and his life and property are guaranteed and protected. Taking his life or violating his property is not permissible; therefore, causing violence, *takfir*, inciting sectarianism and conflict between Muslims are also not permissible. It is necessary to protect revered Islamic figures, and one should be careful not to be abusive to matters that are revered by Muslims. It is not permissible to destroy the dignity of believers and insult them.

Grand Ayatollah Sayyid Muhammad 'Ali 'Alawi Gurgani

آیت الله العظمی سید محمد علی علوی گرگانی دامظله

Brotherhood

Whoever bears testimony (*shahadah*) to the oneness of God and the (messengership of) the Prophet (S) becomes a Muslim, and once he becomes a Muslim, he is a brother of everyone.[50]

One should not persist in taking the road of fomenting division and creating an atmosphere of hostility. This is only to the benefit of international supremacism and Zionism. In the past, different Islamic sects used to come together out of respect despite their own particular ways of thought and live together peacefully. They would simply sit in discussion circles and have rational debates. Today we should also live peacefully with each other and be one united front. What we have instead are *takfiri* groups who, because of their hostility to other sects, especially the Shi'is, use whatever pretence to kill and terrorise Muslims in many places such as Pakistan, Afghanistan, Iraq, Syria, and Indonesia. This is condemnable. These actions of theirs only make the supremacist forces in the world happy and play into their hands.

The enemy is seeking to sow misunderstanding between the two schools of thought, Shi'i and Sunni, through incitement. Therefore, the two sides, whether Shi'i or Ahl al-Sunnah, should not disrespect each other's revered figures. The responsibility of the *maraji'* and the scholars of religion in this instance is to raise awareness (of this issue). For a long time, the Islamic scholars have

---

[50] Remarks by Grand Ayatollah 'Ali 'Alawi Gurgani on the visit of the Head of the Imam 'Ali (A) Consultative Association and a number of students from Georgia, 7 Bahman 1393 (*hijri* solar calendar).

been forerunners in the path of protecting unity among the various branches of the *ummah* of Islam.[51]

We must set things in motion within our own borders and show each other respect and experience good feelings and emotions, because if we depart from the path of impartiality, we will be afflicted by a multitude of troubles.[52]

---

[51] Remarks by Grand Ayatollah 'Ali 'Alawi Gurgani on the visit of Ayatollah Muhsin Araki.

[52] Remarks by Grand Ayatollah 'Ali 'Alawi Gurgani on the visit of the administrative staff of the Hajj and Ziarat Research Centre, 22/1/1392 (*hijri* solar calendar).

GRAND AYATOLLAH HUSAYN MAZAHERI

آیت الله العظمی حسین مظاهری دامظله

Respecting revered figures

Whether done by an individual or a group, fomenting division, inciting sectarian sentiments especially by disrespecting the revered figures and beliefs of Muslims and creating divisiveness among the ranks of the followers of the great Prophet of God (S) are not permissible from a rational and a *shar'i* basis. Similarly, the commission of wanton acts of destruction and suicide attacks by takfirist groups with a rigid and hard-hearted attitude that results in the killing of innocent Muslims is shameful and inhuman, and it would pain the heart of every normal person. There is no doubt that these types of actions are what the enemies of Islam and Muslims desire and welcome.

Disrespecting the revered figures and beliefs of Muslims and creating divisiveness among the ranks of the followers of the great Prophet of God (S) is not permissible on a rational and a *shar'i* basis.[53]

---

[53] See <https://www.tapatalk.com/topic/7090-104498>.

Grand Ayatollah Sayyid Yusuf Madani Tabrizi

آیت الله العظمی سید یوسف مدنی تبریزی ﷻ

Suicide attacks

Islam does not permit showing disrespect towards the beliefs of any religion, especially towards the Islamic schools of thought. Thus any action that would result in divisiveness among the Islamic *ummah* and bring loss, and the destruction of lives and property upon Muslims is forbidden (*haram*) and goes contrary to religious law.[54]

Suicide attacks upon Muslims and killing them in different countries pains the heart of the friend of the *shari'ah* and that of every normal person. These types of actions are not in concordance with Islam as a religion of kindness and mercy; they only efface that image of Islam in the world.

May God preserve and protect the Muslims from the evil of the oppressors and corrupters.

---

[54] See <https://www.tasnimnews.com/fa/news/1393/10/13/60733>.

Grand Ayatollah Sayyid 'Abd Al-Karim Musawi Ardabili

آیت الله العظمی سیدعبدالکریم موسوی اردبیلی ﷾

Sectarian strife

Those who imagine that they can defend Islam with bloodshed and extremism have been duped by becoming tools for the ambitions of the enemies of the Islamic *ummah*. Imam 'Ali ibn Abi Talib (A) held the vilification and disrespecting of others to be impermissible and forbade abusive language. In these turbulent times, the followers of the school of the Ahl al-Bayt (A) should be at the forefront of making peace and reconciliation in the *ummah* against sectarian strife and use the revelatory teachings and guidance of the Messenger of God as a roadmap in their activities.

AYATOLLAH MUHAMMAD TAQI MISBAH-YAZDI

آیت الله محمد تقی مصباح یزدی دامَظِلّهُ

Friendly relations

From the time of Shaykh Tusi until the time of Sayyid Sharaf al-Din, our *'ulama* had relationships and friendly social relations with the Ahl al-Sunnah. In the narrations of the Ahl al-Bayt (A), it has been recommended that we participate with the Ahl al-Sunnah in congregational prayers, attend their funerals, and so on. The Shi'is should have "respectful and cordial relations" with them, should not relate with the [followers of different Islamic schools of thought] with acrimony, and should not vilify their revered figures.[55]

We should institute Shi'i-Sunni unity based on the common facts [that we share], and we should not emphasise instances where there are differences. This is because if the *'ulama* on both sides reject each other because of non-essential issues and lean towards *takfir*, the very edifice of Islam will be destroyed, and Muslims will not be able to live together. It is for this reason that the Ahl al-Bayt (A) recommended that the Shi'is should pray in the mosques of the Ahl-al-Sunnah, visit their sick, participate in their funerals, and even put up with their unkindness. This is a subject that has been stressed.[56]

---

[55] Remarks of Ayatollah Misbah-Yazdi on the visit of the Friday Prayer Leader of Imamshahr City, 25 Dey 1391 (*hijri* solar calendar).

[56] Remarks of Ayatollah Misbah Yazdi during the visit of a number of non-Iranian students, 10/2/1394 (*hijri* solar calendar). See Ayatollah Misbah Yazdi Media Centre <http://mesbahyazdi.ir/node/5570>.

Ayatollah Muhammad Rida Mahdawi Kani

آیت الله محمدرضا مهدوی کنی ﷺ

Question

Recently it has been asked, to whom do Islamic laws apply? Do they apply to all the sects that profess Islam, from Sunnis to Shi'is? Do all of them fall under the laws and rulings of Islam?

Answer

Whoever professes the *shahadatayn* [attesting to the unity of God and attesting to the prophethood of the Seal of the Prophets (S)] is a Muslim unless he has enmity and hostility towards the Ahl al-Bayt of the Prophet (A) and expresses that enmity. The Shi'is of the Ahl al-Bayt (A) are commanded to conduct themselves with all Muslims in a spirit of brotherhood, amicability and sincerity, participate (with them) in their congregational prayers and their funeral services, visit their sick, endeavour to show them love, and be of assistance to them. They are commanded to avoid sectarian behaviour and enmity towards other Muslims; this is what the enemy of Islam desires. The Shi'is are obligated to respect the revered figures of all of the schools of thought (*madhahib*) and be aware of the troublemaking caused the enemy of Islam and Muslims. They cause trouble because they are terrified of the Islamic awakening. Allah says:

و اعْتَصِمُوا بِحَبْلِ اللَّهِ جَمِيعاً وَ لا تَفَرَّقُوا وَ اذْكُرُوا نِعْمَتَ اللَّهِ عَلَيْكُمْ إِذْ كُنْتُمْ أَعْدَاءً فَأَلَّفَ بَيْنَ قُلُوبِكُمْ فَأَصْبَحْتُمْ بِنِعْمَتِهِ إِخْواناً

Hold fast to the rope of Allah altogether, and do not divide. And remember the blessings of Allah upon you when you were enemies, and [Allah] united your hearts, so that you became brethren by His blessing. (Qur'an 3:103)

اللهم انصر الاسلام واهله واخذل الكفر واهله

O Allah! Aid Islam and its people, and disgrace kufr and its people.[57]

Pronouncing *takfir* upon Muslims from whatever group they may be, murdering them, or seizing their property is forbidden (*haram*) and is a mortal sin.

مَنْ قَتَلَ نَفْساً بِغَيرِ نَفْسٍ أَوْ فَسادٍ فِى الْأَرْضِ فَكَأَنَّما قَتَلَ النَّاسَ جَمِيعا

Whoever slays someone – except in punishment for murder or corruption in the land – is as if they have killed all of humanity, altogether. (Qur'an: 5:32)

---

[57] A commonly recited prayer.

Ayatollah Muhammad Yazdi

Chairman of the Council of Experts for the Leadership

آیت الله محمدیزدی دامظله

Statements

Allah says:

$$\text{وَ لَا تَسُبُّوا الَّذِينَ يَدْعُونَ مِنْ دُونِ اللَّهِ فَيَسُبُّوا اللَّهَ عَدْواً بِغَيْرِ عِلْمٍ}$$

Do not insult those they invoke other than Allah, lest they insult Allah in enmity without knowledge. (Qur'an 6:108)

The Noble Qur'an unequivocally prohibits disrespectful language, cursing, and imprecating misguided people, for this action could provoke them into disrespecting the God of the universe out of ignorance. It therefore follows that it is not correct to curse, swear, or use disrespectful language to someone who is held in respect by many people. If such behaviour directly or indirectly results in killings, massacres, the destruction and damage to lives, property or people's honour, it is quite clear that this would be *haram* and goes against *shari'ah* in this world, and in the afterlife one would have to answer for it. It matters not whether this action, this disrespectful language, this cursing, or this imprecating takes the form of a speech, a poem, a eulogy, or even in a lamentation, whether it is presented in theatre, in movie cinematography or whether it is in a real or virtual environment. The form it takes makes no difference for it to be a cause and a factor in leading to killings, massacres, and assaults upon the inviolability of the lives, property and honour of others.

It is not permissible and indeed it is forbidden to curse and imprecate the leaders of the heavenly denominations. This is especially so with respect to the divinely sent prophets but is also true for the caliphs and their successors, and in particular the most notable personalities of Islam which include the wives and offspring of the Prophet (S).

In general, there is no right to curse, imprecate or use disrespectful language at any place, time. It should not have even the smallest role or explanatory effect with respect to elaborating on a subject.

Ayatollah Asif Muhsini

آیت الله آصف محسنی دامظلّه

Statements

1) Whoever believes in the oneness of God, in the messengership of Muhammad al-Mustafa and the finality of prophecy in him and in the Day of Judgment is a Muslim.
2) Violating the life, property, and the chastity of every Muslim is emphatically forbidden (*haram*).
3) A Muslim is the brother of another Muslim. In protecting this brotherhood, it becomes necessary to cooperate with each other in the furtherance of Islam and excuse one's self from getting involved in matters that might cause disagreements between each other.
4) Instigating divisiveness between the adherents of the Islamic schools of thought (*madhahib*) is being treacherous to the religion of Islam.

AYATOLLAH MUHAMMAD MAHDI ASIFI

آیت الله محمد مهدی آصفی ﷺ

Statements

1) Whoever verbally says the *shahadatayn* and acknowledges the divinely ordained laws and necessary rules that all Muslims have consensus upon is counted as a Muslim, and violating his life and property is forbidden. It is narrated in an authentic narration from the Messenger of God (S):

...فإذا قالوها عصموا مني دماءهم وأموالهم إلا بحقها وحسابهم على الله

> ...When [people] say ["there is no God but Allah"], their lives and property will be protected from me. Other than that, the reality of the *shahadatayn* and the account of their deeds are Allah's business.[58]

2) The Messenger of God (S) regarded those who made war upon Muslims and struggled against them without clear *shari'ah* rulings or without being [justified] in the Book and the Sunnah, as *kafir* (unbelievers). On the occasion of the Farewell Hajj when he was at the al-Khayf Mosque in Mina, he said:

إنّ أموالكم ودماءكم وأعراضكم عليكم حرام كحرمة يومكم هذا ، فى بلدكم هذا ، فى شهركم هذا ...

> Indeed your property, your lives and your honour among each other are inviolable (haram) just like the inviolability

---

[58] This narration has been mentioned by Ahmad Hanbal in different sections of his *Musnad*. Bayhaqi has also mentioned it in his *Sunan*, Bukhari and Muslim in their own *sahih* books and a large group of Prophetic *hadith* memorizers from both the Shi'i and Sunni schools with *sahih* chains of narrators.

of today [Eid al-Adha], the inviolability of this month [Dhu al-Hijjah, which is one of the months where fighting and violence was made haram] and the inviolability of this holy land [Mecca].

Then he said:

لاترجعوا بعدى كفاراً يضرب بعضكم رقاب بعض

Do not return to unbelief (*kufr*) after me, some of you smiting the necks of others.[59]

3) Fanning the flames of extremist-originated discord, hatred and causing schisms among Muslims are not permissible. In the same vein, striving to create discord between the united ranks of Muslims, to cause schisms, separation and alienation from each other is also not permissible. God says:

وَاعْتَصِمُوا بِحَبْلِ اللَّهِ جَمِيعاً وَلاَتَفَرَّقُوا

And hold fast to the rope of Allah altogether and do not split. (Qur'an 3:103)

There is no doubt that insulting and disrespecting the revered symbols of Islamic schools of thought is one of the greatest factors that cause schisms which God has forbidden us from doing.

4) Almighty God has commanded us in our interactions with other Muslims, regardless of their sect or their school of thought, with the exception of the Nasibis [those who express hatred for the Prophet's family (A)], to behave kindly towards them, to be pleasant

---

[59] This narration is one about which there is consensus. Ahmad ibn Hanbal mentions it in different sections of his *Musnad*. Nisa'i also mentions it in *al-Sunan al-Kubra*, Ibn Habban in his *Sahih*, and Bukhari and Muslim in their two *Sahih*s. Additionally, a large group of memorizers of the Prophetic *hadith* mention it with *sahih* chains of narrations according to both Shi'i and Sunni traditions in their compilations.

in our behaviour with them, to be affable and cooperative, to integrate with them, to visit each other's sick, and to love them. There are indeed many narrations from the Noble Messenger of Islam (S) that talk of these subjects, and a large number of them are judged to be authentic (*sahih*). Similarly, in the school of the Ahl al-Bayt (A), there are authentic narrations with chains of transmission that are *mu'tabar* (worthy of consideration) that talk about this subject which we have cited in the book *Fitnah al-Ta'ifiyyah*.

5) Whatever we have said above should not be taken to mean that it is a barrier to jurisprudential and theological discussions among the various schools of thought where specialist language is used and when they take place in an intellectual atmosphere of impartiality among Muslim lay and religious scholars. These types of discussions would definitely result in mutual development and growth, and lead to mutual exchanges in culture, jurisprudence, and theology among Muslims. This is what our beloved Islam recommends and encourages us to do.

We ask God Almighty to let us speak with one voice, to give us unity in confronting difficulties and in tackling the issues we have in common, and we ask Him to approve and render successful those who are the forerunners in their advocacy for Muslim unity and convergence between them.

Ayatollah Muhammad 'Ali Taskhiri

آیت الله محمد علی تسخیری دامَظِلَهٗ

Respect

We should show respect for each other's revered figures. Imam al-Sadiq's behaviour with (members of) the other schools of thought was friendly and warm. It is an indisputable fact both in our history and in *hadith* that we should interact with all human beings with love and brotherhood. In narrations attributed to Imam Sadiq (A) he said:

مَنْ صَلَّى مَعَهُمْ فِى الصَّفِّ الْأَوَّلِ كَانَ كَمَنْ صَلَّى خَلْفَ رَسُولِ اللَّهِ ص فِى الصَّفِّ الْأَوَّل

> Whoever prays in the first rank (behind a Sunni imam) is like someone who has prayed in the first rank behind the Messenger of Allah (S).

For this reason, Shahid al-Awwal (may God have mercy on him) says in his textbook that, 'If someone had the option to choose between praying behind a Shi'i imam and Sunni imam, I would choose to pray behind a Sunni imam'. This explication of Shahid al-Awwal – because of his greatness – should not be taken lightly. This religious scholar with such a status and position says that instead of wanting to be present in the congregational prayer of Shi'is, he prefers to be present at the congregational prayers of the Sunnis.[60]

---

[60] Ayatollah Taskhiri in an interview with Shafaqna <http://shafaqna.com/persian/elected/item/133225>.

Ayatollah Muhammad Hashimi Salihi

آیت الله محمدهاشم صالحی دامظله

Muslim unity

Islam has emphasised the unity of Muslims so much that maybe after associating things with God (polytheism) there is no subject [i.e. disunity] that it has forbidden more, to the extent that it has been said:

بنى الاسلام على دعامتين كلمة التوحيد و وحدت الكلمة

> Islam was built upon two pillars: the confession of the oneness of Allah, and unity in the profession to faith.

Therefore violating the lives, property or honour of Muslims is a major sin and is prohibited in the religion of Islam. Furthermore it makes it impermissible to disrespect the beliefs of any religion or sects among the Islamic schools of thought.

From another perspective, suicide attacks against Muslims and their mass killings in various countries are those things that have been divinely prohibited. These are instances of corruption on the earth and unpardonable sins that lead to an eternity in the fires of Hell. All Muslims, including Shi'is and Sunnis, should be vigilant against the plots of the enemies of Islam, schismatic activities, and groups that do *takfir*.

The responsibility of all Muslims is to show the world the true face of Islam, the face of a religion of mercy, love and kindness and a social order based on the principle of 'dispute with them in the best way' (Qur'an 16:125). It is necessary that Muslims cooperate in protecting our brotherhood in the furtherance of Islam.[61]

---

[61] See <http://imam.miu.ac.ir/index.aspx?fkeyid=&siteid=17&pageid=40530&newsview=59568>.

AYATOLLAH MURTADA MUTAHHARI

استاد شهید آیت الله مرتضی مطهری ﷺ

Divisions create weakness

That which befell the Muslims, taking away their power and letting the non-Muslim world victimise them was sectarian divisiveness itself. Without a doubt, the Muslims' need for unity and concord is indeed a most definite need, for a fundamental affliction of the Muslim world is these very old hatreds between Muslim peoples. The enemy is always looking to exploit these.[62]

---

[62] Murtada Mutahhari, *Emamat va Rahbari*, p. 15.

www.ingramcontent.com/pod-product-compliance
Lightning Source LLC
Chambersburg PA
CBHW071745080526
44588CB00013B/2158